REFLECTIONS OF SOARING

BY

The Hawk

All rights reserved.

Copyright © 2004 by Ed "Hawk" Markow

Cover art copyright © 2004 by Ed "Hawk" Markow

No part of this book may be reproduced or transmitted in any form or by any means, electronic or mechanical, including photographing, recording, or by any information storage and retrieval system, without permission in writing from the publisher.

The characters and events in this book are fictitious. Any similarity to real persons, living or dead is coincidental and not intended by the author.

ISBN 1-59146-019-0

Crystal Dreams Publishing

crystaldreamspub.com
P.O. Box 698   Dover, TN 37058

Printed in the United States of America

Crystal Dreams Publishing

Wow

If you found this book satisfying, please investigate the other books that we offer.

Come to http://crystaldreamspub.com and Explore our site and discover the fantastic authors that we are proud to present

TW Miller
Head Publisher
Crystal Dreams Publishing

Introduction

As I worked on this book I thought about how and why it came about. I started writing poetry as a quest to "find" a way to quench my thirst for my own method of artistic expression. I had tried drawing, but even my "stick men" were still stick men when I was done…..but they were ugly! I tried Sculpting, what I wound up with was a lump of clay even more deformed than what I started with. Music? Same results. Then, a very dear friend and poet, Sylence Campbell, suggested poetry, at first I laughed and told her that I hadn't written poetry since the fourth grade, "Roses are red, Violets are blue…..", and that I doubted my ability to do anything poetic. Then one night I was sitting at my desk at home and picked up a pen and started writing, and out it came….within an hour I had written five poems and as I read them back to myself, I came to realize that they were a true reflection of who I am. I was hooked on the art form and nothing could now stop me from expressing myself in this way.

From that time my writing has undergone a myriad of changes and metamorphoses, but through all of it ONE thing remained a constant, everything I wrote was and is a pure reflection of me, I gilded nothing, left nothing out and was honest in exposing much that had been hidden within. To that end I compiled this work not in chronological order, but in virtually no order to allow the reader see who I am without the varnish of the practice and improvement in my art.

What I want for the readers is for them to be able to find something of themselves in my writing, to see and recall how similar circumstances and occurrences affected their own lives, and how they felt about them. Moreover, I hope the readers enjoy this work and feel the emotions that I do as I write.

Acknowledgements

There are so many people to say thank you to for their help and support in my writing.

My family, Mom, Jack, Mark, Marianne and Bill and all of their extended families, my Dad who was and always will be my hero and who is seeing this moment from heaven.

Angie, without whose support I could never have accomplished this or anything else in my adult life, a special thank you to you, Angie.

So many other people who have touched my heart and my life in so many different ways, I am nothing more than a reflection of those things you all let me see and experience, good or bad, and this is what makes me who I am.

Jackie, you are so much of this book that it is hard to separate you and the poetry. That in itself speaks volumes, for you are the poetry and the poetry is you.

56 Years Old

56 years old
and
5 days new

A life of fighting and winning,
And fighting and losing

I looked for it
But I couldn't find it
What was it??

I was an All American Athlete
I was an All American Warrior
I was an All American American

But it was still missing
What was it??

I feared being thought of as an "artistic type"
I tried singing…it sounded ok….but it wasn't ME
I tried painting…my stick men sucked
I tried sculpting….my clay was still a lump of clay
I tried writing….my work was work

And it was still missing
What was it??

I wrote a poem
I found IT!!
And I was born!!

Just 5 days ago

600 miles

Driving west on I80
600 miles to Cheyenne

200 miles of
corn, soy, corn, soy, corn, soy
going by at 74 MPH

Jim Morrison on the CD changer, moaning,
Rider On The Storm
There's a Killer On the Road

Oh man….will this black ribbon
Lead me anywhere I want to be?

Ahhhh….MacDonald's….
Number 6 please…double quarter pounder
WITH cheese, supersize it!

Omaha….400 miles of NOTHING to Cheyenne
Can anywhere with a place named Ogallala
Really be nothing??

Bonnie Raitt ripping at my heart crying
I Can't Make You Love Me
If You Don't

North Platte…125 to…what??
Why the hell am I making this trip??
What's there??
A weekend in heaven….for how long in hell?
A woman so immersed in herself
That there is no room for anyone else

Sorry Succubus….not this bird

Driving East on I80
600 miles to Duh Moines…

<u>A Bad Day</u>

We all have crappy days
Or so we think.

Do yourself a favor
The next time you're having a bad day
Ask yourself this question:
Did anyone shoot at me today?

if the answer is no
Your day ain't all that bad
Because to be shot at
Is a good indication
That the day could be screwed.

And, if no one shot at you,
Then, obviously, you did not get shot
And that is a good thing
Because being shot

Will truly fuck your day up.

A Chance Meeting

I fell in love at 74 MPH
On I-35 – Again!

A Blue Grand Am
Hair like Spun Gold
Eyes so Green you could disappear in them

A smile that could stop your heart
But it defibrillated mine
Her Hoop Earring
Softly caressing her cheek
As will my palms

I wonder if she minds
That I am planning the honeymoon

As I'm signing this goddamned ticket!!

A New Start

Time to start down a new road,
Time to understand that the old one
Just doesn't work any longer.
A new road, a path to freedom awaits.

You are only confined
By the cell you create within.
Nurture freedom and it is yours.
The power is yours, if you accept it.

Before lies the open sky,
See yourself soaring.
Your dreams are the wind
That lifts your wings.

Take what you want,
Accept that which is given
The non-tangible is the only gift
That provides the freedom of flight.

A Page is Turned

We are conceived in an instant
Hopefully in, and of, love
And a page is turned

For 10 lunar months
Three trimesters
Organs, eyes, torso, appendages, hair
And we are purged into
A septic world from the warmth and safety
Of the womb
And a page is turned

For the next year
We suckle at the breast
Are held in love and warmth
Sleep, grow, see, feel, absorb
And one day
We walk, and the world opens
And a page is turned

For the next few years
We expand our horizons

Discovery of our existence
Toys, other creatures, friends,
Books, pictures, sound
Everything is new, shiny, exciting
And a page is turned

For the following days
Voices crack, breasts blossom,
There is fur where there was none
We bond with our peers
And find the differences
Between boy and girl
And a page is turned

For the next period
Responsibility is engrained,
Cars, relationships, music, movies
Loves are found and lost
Our problems unique
We work, we pair, and we create
And a page is turned

For the next minutes
Our existence becomes two
Or three or more lives
Love is defined in our caring
For others, our depth, our moments

Are shared with man and woman kind
And a page is turned

And then, the process slows
Hopefully with another
We suddenly see what was
Obscured by our youth
And exuberance of being
Fur grays or disappears, vision fades
And a page is turned

Some believe that after this
The book is done
The last chapter written and read
But I believe firmly that it is just

Another page that is turned

A Question of Love

Your voice speaks volumes
The softness of it
When you're in love

The joy driven by
The glint of your laughter
Like the tinkle of bells

The heat of your anger
When frustration honed
To a tight edge

As a result of passion
Soul and heartfelt
Opened by insensitivity

And the questioning
Clear incredulity and disbelief
Of the depth of 3 words from me

I Love You

A Vision

Breasts
Well rounded
And succulent

Thighs
So perfectly turned
And creamy white

Rear
Plump but not fat
Pliant and pert

Coif
Feathery soft
Blonde and groomed

I wonder if she's

A fryer, layer or roaster?

Abandonment

One morning I succumbed to the pain.
I gave into it
and wallowed in its
death grip

People I had welcomed
as friends seemed to have
abandoned me
to quell their own fear

This is alien to me
If you are my friend,
I lift my sword to defend you.
Your fear is my enemy
and I will defeat it

Your enemy is mine
and no strength of will
or might of arm
can escape that consequence

And as my friend,
you live in my thoughts, always
you will never be alone

or abandoned

The death grip
was released by
those very thoughts

For a friend
cannot abandon you.
That can only be done
by a mere acquaintance

and those don't merit
your pain, sorrow,
or sword

Analysis

I don't know why we connected the way we did
I have no idea what power drew us together
I can't tell you what forces put you in my path
Moreover, I don't care to explore why and how.

I'll leave analysis to others who are drawn to that
I opt to explore the here and now of our dynamic
To enjoy the time we share with one another
Those moments that we capture together.

You are not meant to be bound by anyone, nor am I
We are meant to know one another at this time
Whatever that brings, I welcome it
I gladly accept what you give, and take no more

Tomorrow will bring what it brings
Yesterday cannot be relived, nor should it
What I offer to you is my desire to hear you
And honesty.

Another Start

Another year has passed.
What is behind, stays behind
Not to be forgotten or rued,
But to be learned from.

A new Dawn has broken.
Bringing with it new hopes
New dreams and aspirations
And promise of better things.

The new year will bring all again.
Joy, pain, love, fear even anger
But all, experience to grow from
For another life page is turned.

I will rejoice in the things
That enter my life, and celebrate
Those that remain from the past
For every bit of that is a gift.

Will there be a new love?
Will there be prosperity?

Those questions will be answered
As I welcome another start.

At The Bar

Sitting on the barstool
2 scotch's down
I watch you go about
What you do

A smile and a beer
For the fat guy in the ball cap

A smile and 2 El Presidente Margaritas
For the bored housewives

A smile, a smirk and Jack and Coke
For the flirty businessman on the make

A smile and 2 something's with umbrellas
For the couple on their way to a movie

A smile, your phone number and another scotch
For the poet

At Your Side

When you feel weak
When you feel vulnerable
See in yourself, what I see.
Strength and conviction – the tower.

You need nothing or no one
You are power personified
Of this, have no doubt,
And know that you are not alone.

For as the gods watch over you,
As the guides light your path
Walk your road with confidence,
I have your back.

Awakening

The awakening hours
When we begin to find
That which is real
Within us and around us

A path illuminated
By the realization of self
The discovery that we need
Very little, but want much

We become secure within
And require nothing from out
Like the butterfly emerging
Blue, yellow, black – born new

We spring upon the landscape
As the equinox is spawned
As the spring evolves
And we are birthed to life anew.

Best Friends

I don't want you to be my best friend.

I lie to my best friend
I tell him that his ex was a bitch
But she wasn't

I don't have sex with my best friend
He has a hairy ass
As far as I can tell, that is!

I don't confide everything
To my best friend,
Just what I want him to know

I don't bring my best friend
Flowers on Friday
Or coffee in bed every morning

I don't want to read the paper
In bed on Sunday morning with him.
I don't like the comics section.

I have no interest
In kissing him
That mustache repels me

I wouldn't give up my other friends
Or my life
For my best friend

But I will for you
Without a second thought.

Blithering Idiot

There are a lot of idiots
In this world.

Assholes, buttheads,
Nincompoops, dumbasses.
All akin, all infuriating.

But…it takes a singular,
And highly specialized talent
To achieve the status of
BLITHERING IDIOT!

Words alone cannot adequately
Describe the talent required
For this title to be affixed.

It is not awarded for one
Solitary act, deed or misdeed,
But for a lifetime of utter
And complete idiocy.

Descriptively, a Blithering Idiot
Is the guy driving a semi truck
70 miles per hour

In a blinding snow storm.

Someone who feeds sharks
By hand (or lack thereof).
A person who volunteers
to umpire a women's softball game.

The contestants on "Fear Factor".
Jerry Springer junkies.
Anyone who drinks kool aid in Jonestown.
A person who joins the army
To be all that they can be.

And my personal favorite
The guy who thinks he's going to get laid
By asking what someone's "sign" is.

And this years Blithering Idiot Award
Goes to……………..

The terrorist who wore sandals
With plastic explosive for soles!!

Brittania

Complexity is your trademark
Hide the vulnerability
Display the hardness
Showcase the enticing

Be louder than the others
Show them the way
Put in more effort
Faster, stronger, better

Give admirers a mere glimpse
Expose the exterior
Tease with abandon
But, No one gets inside the shell

Within is a softness that suffers
Abused by many, including yourself
Few have respected it
Fewer have honored it

Those who should have nurtured it
Need nurturing themselves

So you turn inside
And become the parent

You became mystical and mysterious
Disguised as the druid
Hidden by lurking in Stonehenge
Dancing with the ancients

You fear being wanted
Because you fear dependence
And so you flit like the
Restless one, wandering.

Carpe Diem

Seize the Day

What a perfect concept
It addresses
The way I see my life

I own this day
I make it good
I make it bad
And only I
Can change it

If my day is shit
I made it shit

If my day is great
I made it great

And when you
Are in my life
I'll share my joy

Seize it
And make it yours too

Changes

Life never fails to amaze me
Sometimes I'm given something to ponder
Sometimes I'm given a new challenge
Sometimes I'm given a problem to solve.

Life always puts things in my path
Some thing's make me stumble along the way
Some things make me remember my past
Some things make me want to seek more.

Life takes me to new places
Some places are dark and dangerous
Some places are warm and secure
Some places are exotic and exciting.

Life brings people into my world
Someone who brings happiness
Someone who brings pain
Someone who brings anger.

Life likes to surprise me
It has taken me along a road

It has shown me my errors and successes
It has brought me to this point

And then, life brought me you
It brought light to my darkness
It brought solace to my sorrow
It brought joy, happiness and love.

Life gave me love
Love gave me life

Charles Kuralt Revisited

Interstate 80 to I-76
seven hours of farms
and small towns

Some might say
flat, boring, monotonous
not I

For the land
weaves its own tapestry

In spring
it is miles of a veil
of barely perceptible
striking green atop
rich dark chocolate earth

In summer
it is an endless sea
of waving green arms
topped by the golden tassels
of the coming harvest

In autumn
a mottled carpet
of brilliant reds,
fiery orange, pale yellows
and earthy browns

and in winter
a blanket of virginal white
broken only by leafless
oaks and scrubs
waiting for spring
to come to life again.

I-76 to I-70
three hours of rolling knolls
and cattle ranches

Cowboy Country
called by many
I see it differently

Groups of Bovines
meandering slowly towards
an unseen goal, perhaps a meal,
or standing grazing and gazing
protectively over
spindly legged calves, shiny and new

Another symbol of
the ongoing cycle of life
our rebirth

I-70 to I-15
about eight hours of
stark contrast between
man and God

The symbols of man,
cities, ski lodges, resorts
and those of God

From snow covered slopes
dotted by pine and aspens
almost fouled with the
Machinery that deludes the puny humans
that they have conquered this majesty

To the Majesty
of canyons and arroyos
of Red and Tan Monuments
assuring the same humans
that they were here long before
and will remain here long after

They almost imperceptibly
give way to, and indeed become
the towering rock formations,
sand and scrub
of the high desert

Majestic, powerful and steadfast
these mountains and valleys
stand in proud solitude
and take no notice
of my awe of them

I-15 to I-5 to the sea
the last seven hours
of my journey west

Miles of desert valley floor
foothills sitting solemnly on them
quiet, but still teeming with life
occasional cacti, brush and tumbleweed
staid, proud, determined

The garish glow
of neon and the facade
of what man foolishly deems wealth
so illusory and temporary
stands surrounded by the desert

For permanence is demonstrated
only by these fleeting images
that have guided and sung to me
along this quest

From farmland to mountains
from foothills to desert
and ultimately, to the sea

I come away from this trip
with a profound respect
of the true majesty
of the strokes from the paintbrushes
and hand moldings of
Gods artwork

and a deeper understanding that
this was but one small part
of Gods Palette

Choices

Life is a very short journey
It is meant to be lived
Not to be simply observed
I will live mine in fullness

She who chooses to participate
Will be welcomed and fulfilled
She who does not will be forgotten
Get in the boat or swim away

I do not accept simple observation
That is MY choice, my option
Be part of that choice
Or move on your decision

I don't force your choices
I respect your options
Don't ask me to support them
It is YOUR life – choose wisely

Creativity

Is my art good??
Who cares
It's mine
Will anyone ever see it
Or care about it?
Doesn't matter.

Am I conveying anything of meaning??
Sure I am
To me.

This is my self portrait
A piece of my soul
I don't need your approval

To make me whole.

Crossroads

We have agreed to disagree
You have what you want
I cannot have what I want
Right, wrong or indifferent

The die has been cast
The paths have been chosen
Irrespective of how and why
We shall never know

I detest the outcome
But I cannot/will not alter it
We will remain unseeing
For our paths have split

There are but two roads
One is growth, the other is death
Without embracing the first
The second is all there is.

Cycles

Watch the sun rise and set sometime.

Has man ever created
an orange so brilliant
as to match the fire of a dawn
aflame and pressing against
the blue, shading to black
of a dying night?

What artist has captured
the purples. mauves and tangerines
of night in pursuit of
the day, as it ends
its journey

It's all so representative
NOT of beginnings and endings
But of that never-ending cycle

The Renewal of Life

Dance Naked For the Fools

Dance naked for the fools
Seduce them with empty promises
Tempt them with your smile
Hypnotize and draw forth the dream

Sway like wisps of smoke
Drawn around the ceiling fan
Quiver with feigned excitement
Slink across the stage and beckon

Beam the enticing stare
Reveal the external shell
Exotic siren luring,
Eliciting erotic fantasy

Allude to all deliver nothing
only hyper dreams and hope
keeping you for yourself,
and one who knows.

Darkness

Darkness welcomes me
It provides enveloping comfort
Drawing me into the eddy's of sleep
Enfolding me into its arms

Here I find my haven
From garish reality
The stark harshness of waking
Captured in the yoke of awareness

The inky black is my tabloid
From which springs the fabric
That is weaved into my mantle,
My cloak of consciousness

This is the labyrinth
That defines my words
That gives birth to the thought
And forms my poetry.

Dilemma

He looks within, confused
Torn between what he feels
And what he knows is right
To go, to stay, to live the lie.

He does not feel love for them
He loves the comfort in their arms
He finds rapture and ecstasy
Yet, with her, he feels love.

The passion died a quiet death
Many years ago, amid sorrow
He knows they are all temporary
And cares not, for there are others.

Yes, he knows his shallowness
But takes comfort in knowing
That all find peace in this
Nights of passion, days of caring.

Disgust In Reality

We have reached new heights
In our tribute to stupidity.
We are all guilty by association
We are the rats B.F. Skinners maze.

Reality TV is the evidence.
For a pitiful amount of money
Contestants betray confidences
Shared with them, call a person
A friend and then turn on them,
Singing "Its part of the game!"

They eat disgusting items,
Portend to perform
"Death Defying" feats,
challenging ones sensibilities,
"Survive" the "wilds",
endure inane lie detector tests.

They even marry a "partner"
They don't have any way of knowing,
And then part, when they discover

The "mate" is as fucked up
As themselves.

Worse yet, we are manipulated
As are the rats in the maze
Or the public in the "fantasy"
Of George Orwell's "1984".

Think about it,
"games" devised by the "haves"
to entice the "Have nots"
a dangling carrot,
the "cake" offered by
a self centered "queen"

we can only truly win
when we refuse to play.
Better yet, when we refuse
To be participatory or exercise
Our voyeuristic proclivities.

Become More,
Create rather than appease
Grow and learn
Covet what we can gain from each other
Share and be true to what is truly gold
Humankind.

Don't Ask

Don't ask if your song
is melodious
it is - if you sing it

don't ask if your story
has depth and meaning
it does - if you are inspired

Don't ask if your art
moves someone
It will - if you are moved

Don't ask if your poetry
expresses emotion
it does - if you feel it

Don't ask if someone loves you
They do
If <u>you</u> love you

Emailgasm

I used to bitch
About junk mail
Before the internet

But I would welcome
Anything less than
200 emailgasms a day

I don't need or want:
A $10,000 dollar a week
Work at home job. A new
Hair Removal system.
A new hair restoral system,
A free cell phone or
Seven trillion free minutes.

Viagra, vigel, or bigger breasts.
A new penis, a larger penis
Or anyone else's penis.
Girls "doing" other girls,
Animals, cars, boats, planes,
Trains, or other mysterious objects
Or people. Oh yeah,
Let us not forget hentai!

No loans, mortgages or
Debt relief. Most of all
I don't want ANY free memberships
To anywhere, place, thing or site.

Please God,
Put more shit in my
Snail mail box!

Emergence

A new and brighter day is beginning to emerge.
I was unaware of how I had cloaked emotions
Buried under the shroud of doubt
And hidden from all, including myself.

Examination of the cause is relevant
If only to learn from the past
The impetus is on stepping forward
And braving the unknown.

I accept the challenge being presented
To expose the core of my existence
To drop my shield and allow
Feeling to flow unimpeded by fear.

I stand naked before the truth
Ready to venture into the morrow
To face the unknown exposed
Leaving that cold, drab cocoon behind.

Error

I sat musing the other day
And I recalled, with sorrow,
The loss of one I had loved.

Those days of holding
Onto one another
The nights assimilated
And enmeshed in passionate embrace
The mornings, awakening
Enfolded together

Then, reality broke in rudely
And other memories took form.
Our anger with each other
Voices crackling like
The electricity of our synapses firing

Her inability to reach out
My reluctance to accept
The sterility of our
Mutual understanding that
The "love" was a pretense

A misspelling of a simple word

LIKE

Escape Artist

Escape Artist, what are you running from?

Houdini had nothing on you.
You have made escape
A way of life.

Sadly, what you leave behind
Is pain that almost
Equals your own.

Worse yet,
Some of what is left
Can help ease your pain.

Are you afraid of being harmed?
Are you running from someone?
Are you running to someone?
Are you afraid of what you may find?

If you stop
You might be hurt.
If you stop

You may find what you seek.
If you stop
You may begin to heal

And you will discover
That what you run from
Cannot be escaped from

Because
You can't escape from yourself

Fame in A Fog

Poetry written in a bar
Songs written through a haze

Morrison, Joplin, Hendrix, Presley
Love spoken in pain

Gaye, Darren, Bruce, Hemingway
Creation in Purgatory

Monroe, Belushi, Mansfield, Duncan
Artistic in perpetuity

Gone so soon
Away so long
Yet here forever

Feel It

Some people make things happen
Others wait for them to happen
Still others wonder
What the fuck happened!

Wait?? For What??
For someone else to decide?
Me follow another? NO WAY!!
I write my own music, consequences be damned.

Those who wait are doomed
Never to experience.
Without pain, there can be no joy
Give life to your senses

Take the leap
Step out onto the edge
Look over and fear not
The worst that can happen is the best

You might discover
That you are alive.

Laws of Physics

For every action
there is an equal
and opposing reaction

Toss a rubber ball
against a wall
and it bounces back to you

How many of us
see how that applies
to the aspects of our lives?

When we express anger
towards another
they express either anger or fear

In relationships
we express love
and that love is returned

and when we hate
how can anything but hate
be reciprocated??

Equal and opposing
Choose your poison---or pleasure

For Jackie

An Enigma, paradoxically endowed.
A first look provides one view
it says much, but it says nothing
tonight's reality, a diaphanous veil
revealing less than it appears to.

Time and trust chips away the cover,
But only as much as YOU allow.
I am convinced that I see
Beyond what you allow the masses
I envision a goal orientation.

But the goal is unspecific
Other than "Freedom"
Perhaps it is the goal
and it is the route that remains
unspecific, maybe unclear.

You question Yourself, asking,
Can I continue in this world,
A world existing in the night
Occupied by denizens of the dark?
There is comfort in Adoration.

But too many want much more.

Too many would bind you
And keep freedom beyond arms reach
So the Enigma is birthed,
What you see, is not what you get.

A second path is there too
this path can be set upon
by achieving the material metal
that allows you to escape
and seek other places and faces.

The Paradox is that burning need
To be YOU, but not knowing
Absolutely, Who YOU are
The question that gnaws,
"Is this ME or HER?"

I see your strength.
I always have, my wish for you,
is for you to see it too.

For You, Who Understands

As the hawk soars
And weaves his skyline tapestry
As the dolphin glides
Cutting her aqua path

As Orion streaks across the sky
Trailing streamers of comets aglow
As the full moon illuminates
And lends day to the night

As the forest blankets earth
Providing her protective cloak
As mother ocean ebbs and flows
Giving and taking the sands of time

As the song of your soul
Stirs you to dance,
So is our friendship,
Free, unfettered and endless.

Free Will

I heard someone bemoaning
The departure of a lover
And rail about how unfair it was
After all, he had done EVERYTHING for her.

As I listened, I wanted to shake him
And say, "Your free will was to hold,
While hers was to be free."
One cannot do for another.

One can only support another's dream
Be there when you are wanted
And let them follow their own path
As you follow yours.

If these paths converge,
If you are on them together,
Share the journey, each unto each,
And follow your free will

Friday Night

Friday Night, Barstool number 1
Busy Restaurant
Week is over, time for fun

Barkeepers and wait staff
Running to keep up
Cooks and kitchen help needing a laugh

Diners talking, cell phones ringing
Manager smiling mentally taking the tab
Drinkers are drinking….the waiting is fine

The weeks finest moment is here
No bitchy boss, no pissy clients
I'd had enough….how 'bout more beer??

Good News, Bad News

I have good news
And I have bad news

The good news is
I don't hate you
I don't have time for hate
In my life

The good news is
I'm not angry with you
Anger is an emotion
That weakens us

The good news is
I'm no longer saddened
By your absence
Sadness is self defeating

The bad news is
I just don't care
The opposite of love
Is not hate

Its indifference

Acrostic Poetry - Sylence

Standing as our muse
Yielding only to her own obsessions
Lending her skills to those who want to learn
Endlessly supporting our efforts
Nothing seems to deter her from Shadow Poets
Creatively urging, constantly providing motivation
Emotionally tying each of us our art

Hidden Agenda

We banter back and forth
Holding a noisy veil, covering
What no other person
Is allowed to see.

Expose the barbs and thorns
Conceal the vulnerability
Within this cloak of invisibility
But, you see, I see.

We even mask it from
One another – afraid
Of what it might be
unwilling to accept possibility

bound by conventional thought
two rebels caught in a vortex
unable to move in ANY direction
unwilling to stand still.

Hypocrisy

Art imitates life
A trite and overused statement
But so true

I offer a television series,
SURVIVOR,
As my example

We as a society
Have way too often
Forsaken our brothers and sisters

We have forgotten
That nothing is as important
As our fellow humans

Today we honor deceit,
Dishonor, greed and selfishness
By calling it entertainment.

We happily reward
People who lie.
People who have zero concept of friendship.

And then we hold them up
To the world and say,
"Lo, worship them, for they are winners"

Bullshit.
They are losers.
And so are we

For honoring
That which is
Without honor.

I Care

It is true that in my recent past
There have been so many others.
This is not a statement of boast
But one of my shame.

I justified my conquests
By disavowing all knowledge
Of the word "Love"
And stayed devoid of emotion.

Until now, this moment in life,
With my heart naked and exposed
Willing to accept, wanting to give,
Immersed in raw emotion.

I have but two things to present
First is my promise, to be true.
Second is equally important
It is...my love for you.

I never used that phrase
I avoided it like the plague
Those three simple words
That I use today...I love you.

Revelation

I walked into the bright sunlight
And felt the stabbing pain of the light
Shocking me into the reality
That had been hidden by the darkness

The darkness was an illusion
Self created, self perpetuated
Not the inky black of night
But a blurred and dim vision

The reality was stark
And naked in the sunlight
The things I wanted most
Were right in the forefront

Dimmed and blurred by my own volition
The seeking of what was
Missed by looking beyond
And thus almost lost

Insight

Years spent in a self imposed purgatory
did not create bitterness
they gave birth to a new persona
one who loves the mystery of life.

An understanding of essentials
Was birthed by this monastic style
A calmness resides within me,
smoldering rather than in conflagration.

Rage vaporizes and gives way
to an icy cold place in my heart
an internalized immunity to pain
as opposed to externalized anger.

There is no blame leveled at another
nor regret of the past
a small sorrow of what WAS
But greater joy of what IS.

Into The Night

Wild and free we ride into the night,
The cares and concerns left far behind.
This is our moment, this is our time.
Wind in our faces, stars our canopy.

Into the woods, alongside the river,
We lie together in the flickering flame
Warmed by the fire and each other
Nothing exists but nature and we.

Can this be so, can it be real?
Nothing to hide, nothing to fear
We are as one, lying together,
Living this instant as if no tomorrow.

We will take this highway
And journey this path
Never look backward
Just you, me and the wind.

For Jen

A paradox, she is many women
In one woman, a blend of so much
On one side, wildly exotic
On another, universal earth mother.

Like a fine diamond, crafted with skill
She presents many facets
And each is remarkable on its own
And, diamond like, she sparkles.

She fills a room with her energy
And darkens it as she broods,
But never unkind or boorish
She smiles and lights the world.

The teasing dancer
The devoted, loving mother,
The woman who yearns
For a loving touch and words of care.

Beyond what any other knows
She shares her innermost self
And deserves admiration and respect.
She has mine, she is my friend.

Jose Cuervo – My Fiend!

I sat and chatted with my very close friend
Jose Cuervo last night.
I go to him whenever I need a confidant
To commiserate with!

Our conversations always begin
With my tale of woe or joy
Soon he makes me feel a bit lightheaded
And more talkative than normal

I seem to be louder and laugh more
Early in our discussions
But after about an hour
I begin to have some difficulty being clear

Before long, my words appear in disarray
He becomes blurred in my vision
And I begin to feel frustrated
In his difficulty in understanding me

The room begins to spin a bit
And vertigo strikes when I try to
Maneuver to the rest room
Goddamn, this floor is uneven

My stomach begins to feel queasy
And I'm a bit pissed about something
Although I cannot say exactly what
Sumbitch, I think I'm going to be sick!

Maybe if I just lie down for a bit
The room will stop acting like the angry ocean
Blackness envelopes me
And the conversation reaches a lull

Hours later I curse that demon
When I awake to an indescribable pain
And an unquenchable thirst
Even my hair hurts and I feel like I'm dying!

Jose, you're a bastard…leave me alone!!

Journeys

We walk through life
Looking ahead to what might be

We dream of where
Things will be different

And better

And in that journey
We too often forget

To partake of the beauty
That surrounds us

And makes this moment spectacular

Last Night

We've known each other for a while now
Shared some moments, and a lot of each us
With one another, almost daring to be different
We got past the "club/customer" very quickly.

We each sense something else in the other
Neither knows what, but we both enjoy it
A bond of sorts grows, and we gingerly explore it
Baby steps in a budding friendship.

Last night was different, in a good sense.
We, as always, explored a dozen subjects
But something else pushed to a new plateau
I don't know what, I don't analyze, I just experience.

I like the way you challenge my thinking
You like that I listen to you
We both like this level of comfort
And the ease in which we can trust.

In some ways, I think you are older than I

In other ways, you're comforted by my experience
Science calls this a Symbiotic relationship
I simply find joy in it.

Le Petit Mal

"le petit mal"
The Little Death
Strange that we equate
This beginning with the end

I do not accept death as final
It is merely a new path
Another road to travel
A journey yet untaken

Perhaps it is the simple beauty
Defined by the phrase
The word picture painted
By the hand of the poet who penned it

Maybe therein lies the truth
The depth of meaning in the saying
For, le petit mal,
Is another name for an orgasm.

Limbo

Literally, limbo means
Hem or edge.

Writers have given
It broader meaning.
As a state of confinement
Or exclusion.
The prison of the mind.

Theologians reason that
It is a state of non-grace
A placement for those
Whose sin does not merit punishment?
But whose goodness does not merit reward.

And all of these define
A life bereft
Of loving
Or being loved.

I found my limbo.
Loved by one
I am not in love with.

And in love

With one who
Cannot love anyone.

Between heaven and hell.

In a state of Limbo.

Look Inside

Look inside yourself
And find the truth.

A relationship ends
And we feel such depth
Of pain.

Is that pain from
the loss of the other person?
The loss of that togetherness?
Or is it something else?

Perhaps a foreboding sense
That we aren't deserving
Of the closeness.

Or that we aren't
"good enough" or
the other person finally saw
the "real" us.

Worse yet
That we are not
Worthy of love.

We wind up injured,
Broken, tearful.
Those make way
for anger, bitterness, spite.

Until we come to
A healing moment
When we accept
Ourselves.

And do it again!

Love

Love is interesting emotion.
In it
We go from the heights of exaltation
To the very bowels of depression.

We willingly would give up
Our breath
To receive it
As we give it.

We dream of living
Two souls
Enmeshed and intertwined
As one.

And yet when we have it
We quake with fear
At the thought of losing it
And question whether we
Should give it fully

And when it is over
We ask
What the hell was it

That I saw in them?

Marking Time

Caught in the vortex of life
Almost at a standstill.
Where am I going?
How and when will I get there?

Universe, light my path
Help me move toward something,
Give me meaning and hope
That define my goals

Don't let me wallow
In vacant association
With those who do not see
Open my eyes, keep me whole.

There is more, I know there is
I have accomplished much,
I want and need more
I will find what I seek.

A Tribute To Ms. Ego

Hello my dearest friend
Thy name is mirror
But, in you I see grace,
Beauty and such warmth.

Warmth that exceeds that
When once said beauty
Launched a thousand shits
OH MY, I meant ships!

I am clueless as to why
Unworthy souls with untalented
Wit would find you self absorbed,
Snobby or shallow

The unwashed many don't deserve
One so perfect in every way
One sculpted by the finest artist
One so refined and delicate

Why, I'll wager that when
You break wind or defecate
The aroma of freshly cut roses
Delicately caresses your senses

And your voice……
A song from the finest voiced diva
God, I love me so
But why shouldn't I??

After all…I am perfect

I said so!!

Milliseconds

When so much Dark surrounds you,
A mere pinpoint of light
Is like a glaring laser flash
You life is momentarily bright.

Akin to walking from a cave,
Dark and dank, foul and evil,
into BLINDING sunlight
and then it fades....

What was brilliant dims
into shadows and then inky black.
Blinded again, yet almost comforted
by the normality of nothingness.

Is illuminating Joy so short of duration?
Is Ebony, vapid life so bleak??
The "Norm" is a vacuum
Devoid of hope and dreams.

We ask why and why not
Like one deprived of sight
Seeking but not finding
The comfort of the Light

My Memories Of You

The depth of blue in your eyes
Warms me to my core
As I brush back a wisp of your hair

The faint smile that graces your lips
As you awaken
And see me looking at you
Love and wonder in my heart

The quiet hush that falls
As your breathing slows
And then deepens
As Morpheus welcomes you

The silkiness of your skin
The softness of your caress
The sweetness of your kiss

The loneliness of your absence

My Name

I was spawned
In the bowels of Hell.
I've been called Evil Incarnate.
Demons cower where I tread.

The River Styx is my Riviera
The hounds of hell, my pets.
The skull and crossbones
Is my symbol of peace.

I devour the heart of the beast
And grin at his agony
I drink gasoline as my beverage
And piss flames.

I will steal your soul
At the first sign of weakness
And feel absolutely no remorse.
My name is – LOVE.

Mysticism

The magic of divination
Painted by the cards of the Tarot
Major and Minor Arcana
Together illuminate our future.

The stones of the Runes
looking forward and back
Gebo and Sohweilu guiding us
Fehu and Thurisaz protecting

I-ching brings the wisdom
of the ancients to bear
Invoked by three coins juxtaposed
by our own energy

Astrological Guidance
provided by the positions of
Celestial bodies at the very instant
Of our birth, do foretell our morrow.

Pythagorean theorem gives
Depth to numerological sight
Into who we are and why

A mathematical path to follow.

These few methods are gifts
Bestowed upon us to help
Guide and explain, just as
all of our gifts are.

The Goddess smiles on us.

Choices

We make many choices in our lives
Some bad, some good, some we shouldn't
We carve our own destiny
By choosing well each day,
Finding our true path.
Laughter and tears
Flowing free
Heal souls.
Ours.

Promises

Promises made, promises broken
The words we spoke only token
Never knowing what we seek
No depth to what we speak
A lie told by one
Truth is no fun
Leave today
Our way
Weep.

Once Again

I watched the news tonight
We're going to war again

More 19 year olds, just beginning to live
Being pre-fitted for body bags
For What???

Hussein? Bin Laden? Oil? Money? Power?
North Korea, Iraq, Afghanistan
Another Vietnam?

435 Congress Persons
100 Senators
A President, Vice President And an entire Cabinet

Yet only 3 have people
Going in Harms Way

More names on another wall
But none of theirs

How about yours

One Word - Adventure

Adventure – just the word
Brings such delicious thought
To mind.

An image of standing atop
A hill, above a dense forest
Watching an eagle soar over
The canopy of trees below.

Standing at the bow of sailing
Ship, being tossed by a wild
And wind blown sea, sails
At full billow.

Seeing the sun rise over
The foothills, red and gold,
And bringing light to
The expanse of the desert.

One night, in the back seat
Of dads '57 Chevy
With Donna, the strawberry
Blonde from my Spanish class

Delicious thoughts indeed.
Each with their own excitement
And each an adventure!

One Word - Coconut

From the white sand
Of a tropical beach

Springs the coconut palm
Curving sensually inland coaxed by
The caress of the trade winds

Within the thick green husk
Protected by an almost impenetrable shell
Lies meat, crunchy yet delicate

But the pearl to be found
Lies deep within
Sweet and viscous, creamy and white

The milk of the coconut
A tropic delight

One Word - F**K

The MOST versatile word

F**k this
F**k that
F**k me
F**k you

F**kin "A" right
F**k if I know
F**k if I care
F**k it, it don't mean nuttin

F**K yes
F**k no

What the F**k
Why the F**k
Where the F**k
How the F**k
When the F**k

Who the F**k cares???

You do!!!!

Versatility

SHIT – one of the most versatile words I know

Used for emphasis of pain –
SHIT, I stubbed my toe!!

An expression of joy –
Man…..you're the SHIT!!

To denote disgust
This tastes like SHIT!

A spoken threat
I'll kick the SHIT outta you!

Or the ultimate in pleasure
THIS is some good SHIT!!

Yeah, TRULY versatile

NO SHIT

One Year

One year ago yesterday
I thought my life was over
April 11, 2002.

My lover at the time
Terminated her pregnancy
And our baby was gone.

In my life
I have had broken bones
Numerous cuts and contusions
Even been shot……twice

But Nothing prepared me
For pain like that.
The darkness was total
And all encompassing.

Months went by
Some were meaningless.
But, then,
A light began to shine

And that light grew
And brightened

Until it became the sun.

You see,
I realized that our child,
My daughter, exists.

Do not feel sorrow for me.

For that beautiful child
Lives in my heart

And she always will

Our Magic

Our magic is apparent, but only to us
Nothing or no one else matters.
We found something sacred
And in it we will rejoice.

Our pasts are long gone
Though they cannot be erased
Together we will overcome them
For in us there is strength.

We'll walk into tomorrow
Knowing no fear, for what was
Our pain is now our power
Our love is our bond.

We will write of this together
And sing our song as we go
For it is only a moment
Until we ride wild and free.

Paradox

You are a paradox
Much like the chameleon
At one moment, you hate what you do
At another, you love it.

You know that you are meant
For far loftier pursuits
But, at this moment, the ends are justified
Though far beneath your capability.

The biggest reward here
Is the center spotlight
The focus on you, the perspective
That you are the only one in the room.

Balancing between the poles is easy for you
Adaptability is your long suit
You accept the moment, for the moment
And welcome change for the sake of change.

As the serpent sheds its skin
And becomes fresh and new
You continually grow and change

And leave behind what cannot accept.

Like the way a serpent eats
Only when it needs sustenance
You, too, nourish your spirit
And then move forward to the next step.

Stay that path, enigma.
Welcome what comes your way?
Hold onto the magic of your evolution
Explore experience, learn, reach again.

Paths

From my path, they attempt to draw me.
That which is good, beckons to be joined.
That which is evil, tempts me to stray.
That which is right, lights the path.

From my path, I will not be deterred.
Without good, I am lost and in pain.
Without evil, I am blinded to hazard.
Without a path, I am doomed to wander aimlessly.

My path is what I follow to the goal.
Good guides my right and humbles me.
Evil bounds my left and humanizes me.
The path provides me choice.

The path is lit by the conflict.
Good is essential for my life.
Evil is always present and just as necessary.
Polar opposites stir the realization of my path.

There are no absolutes.

A Picture of You

Like a tornado you whip me to a frenzy
Like a siren you beckon me to join you
Like the Muse you inspire me to create

Like the bowsprit you lead me into the tempest
Like the Madonna you watch over me
Like Venus you beguile me

Yet

Like the Ice Princess you chill me
Like the Succubus you draw me
Like the Vixen you fool me

Like the Wench you taunt me
Like the Temptress you summon me
Like the Witch you enchant me

NOW

Just Love Me

Power

Awaken Americans!!

I hear our voices every day
saying "We have no power".

How wrong that is.
The only REAL power
is ours.

The proof is irrefutable.
That power was exercised
in the 60's and 70's

A war was ended
A reign of corruption was ended
Decades of impotence was ended

The poets called to us with power
The musicians sang to us with power
The writers wrote to us with power

And the people of America
Held the power

We must not

Go quietly into that good night

The power is ours

Preparation H

There are pods of whales
And murders of crows
Herds of horses and cows
Even packs of dogs

But here, tonight
We have a gaggle of assholes
You know the type
Ogle, fondle, but NEVER spend

They talk endlessly
But say nothing
I wonder if <u>they</u> work for free
They expect you to

There is a cure for this malady
It will work with just one dose
A simple application
Just a little Preparation H

Purpose

I do not believe that we were put here
To be sad or hurt or angry.
Our purpose is to find the joy,
To seek it and revel in it.

Yes, it not always easy to see
But it is VERY easy to avoid it
And far too many of us
Choose avoidance over acceptance.

We are surrounded by signs of joy
Most of it hidden in plain view
The first robin of spring,
The first snowflake of winter.

Instead, we bask in the cruelty of others
Ignoring our own culpability
In allowing the perpetration of pain
And then, we become artistic about it.

We paint, sculpt, sing and write odes to it
We wallow in the self aggrandization
Of what another did to us.
Bullshit, we did that ourselves.

Accepting our own guilt in the process
Is the first step in total healing
And the first move toward our true goal
The nirvana of discovery of purpose.

A Question Of Love

Your voice speaks volumes
The softness of it
When you're in love

The joy driven by
The glint of your laughter
Like the tinkle of bells

The heat of your anger
When frustration honed
To a tight edge

As a result of passion
Soul and heartfelt
Opened by insensitivity

And the questioning
Clear incredulity and disbelief
Of the depth of 3 words from me

I Love You

Rachel

Externally – an ode to beauty and grace
From delicately turned ankles
Up a sensual path of perfectly formed
Erotically long sultry legs

Hips carved stoically for lovemaking
Beneath a belly so softly firm
To breasts sculpted by the hand of god
And atop silky shoulders, Aphrodite's face.

Internally – Resides the child, impetuous
Jeans and tee-shirt attitude
A hardness forged by the fire
Of an innocence lost

Far older than her years would indicate,
Is this from lives past lived?
Or the rush to live this one?
It matters not – for she is she.

Rage

Rage against that which binds us.
Feed the fury growing within
Break the bonds of repression
That enslaves our souls.

We have enabled our captors
Given them the power to hold us
By being enamored of material goals
Toys – all temporary, all unfulfilling

We seek them so deeply
That we abandon that which is true
The freedom of the wind and sun
The endless flow of river to the sea.

Look to the creatures of earth and sea
Our brothers and sisters in existence
For the lessons of life's joy
Recapture what has been stolen.

Rain

First you sense it coming
The air is heavy...it smells damp

Then you feel it
Was that a drop of water against my face?

Then you hear it
A drop against a leaf, the window, the roof

Then it grows
Tapping, singing the song of freshening

Then it reaches maturity
A crescendo drawing with it the foul and dank into the ground

Then it slows
And you hear the individual drops again

And it stops
The air is heavy...and it smells clean and new and fresh

It's the same everywhere
The Jungle...it brings life

The Desert... it cools
The Forest... it calls forth the spirits
The City... it cleanses
The Rivers, Lakes, Oceans... it joins its brothers and sisters

And is reborn
As we are

Rediscover

When you awake tomorrow
KNOW it is the beginning.
You belong to you and none other
Accept yourself and responsibility
For your own happiness

Arise and dance to the music of life
Sing the song of your freedom
Let your soul light your path
And allow your heart to follow it
No one can take this from you

Capture this exquisite moment
Bask in the warmth of it
Give your dreams flight
Let them soar like the eagle
Fan the flames of tomorrow.

Remembrances

When a relationship ends,
why do we seem to be
able to remember only the pain?

It's almost impossible
to recall the agony
of a broken bone or a wound
in our past

Why is it so hard to recall
that joy we shared
or the comfort
we provided to one another?

I remember your smile sometimes.
I recall your warmth against me
in the night.

But most of all
I remember the goodbye

like it happened today

Rhyming Scheme

In my short poetic life I've known
That I was sorely lacking and alone
And last night as I slept
Into my mind this thought crept

I MUST attempt a rhyming scheme this night
But The Hawk in fear is a terrible sight
I could simply flee the ShadowPoets door
Or try and try and try some more

I hurt my feeble brain as I continued to seek
Those words to pen, afraid to peek
Then these came almost seeming
That I wrote them, but I was only dreaming

Robin

Riding, red hair streaming in the wind
On the back of a stallion, black as the ebony night
Born to be this free, unfettered and wild
In control of the untamed, His mane and tail flying
Nothing to confine them, they move as one.

In those moments of doing what she must
She allows herself to be bound
Inside, she remains free, never held still
Streaking through this world, ultimate rider.

Sacrifice

Words are our own biggest enemy
We use them to conjure false images
Treat them with so little respect
And act like we can unring the bell.

Do not say "I would do ANYTHING,
For this person". It is a lie.
Would you sacrifice EVERYTHING?
We would sacrifice relatively little.

Could you sacrifice your life?
Nice to say, but, unlikely.
Would you sacrifice your child?
We say no, but we do. To abuse.

We sacrifice portions.
A piece of our heart, our mind,
Our self respect, and worse,
Far too much of our soul.

Choose words carefully
They cut deeper than the knife,
Burn hotter than the flames of hell,

And once said, they cannot be unsaid.

Second Chances

You want a second chance to do what?

Lie to me?
Hurt me?
Use me?

Kill me?
Cheat on me?
Abuse me?

Laugh at me?
Misunderstand me?
Accuse me?

BITE ME!

Seeking and Finding

I looked in many places
For my answer
It was nowhere to be found

I turned to many
To replace the loss
Of the irreplaceable

I held so many
In hope of feeling
They were faceless and
Left me empty

I began to find solace
In the solitude
Of my fortress

I kicked myself in the ass
And it appeared
Just a glimpse at first

It grew and took form
It blossomed
And I found my answer

In me, of me, by me, with me

And the healing began

Sensuality

Buffalo wings with Ranch Dressing
Potato Skins with Bacon and Cheese

A Cheeseburger with Grilled Onions
French Fries drenched in Catsup

Tomato and Onion slices with crumbled Bleu Cheese
In a Balsamic Vinaigrette

Blood Rare Prime Rib wit Horseradish Sauce
Baked Potato with Butter, Sour Cream and Chives

Cheesecake, creamy to the palate
A cup of Black Coffee

NOW THIS IS LOVE!!!!

Serpent

The eyes have been long described
As fearful, probing and deathlike.
In reality they are all seeing.
A highlight of slow sensuality.

The eyes smolder with silent passion
Seeking and finding, captivating
Drawing one into their depth
Holding them there until the soul is owned.

They are not cold and lifeless
Sensuality rushed is meaningless
Unhurried enjoyment speaks of life,
Life seized and drawn within.

The serpent speaks of strength
Total adaptability to their ecosystem
Being of it and in it
Feed, spawn, draw the line of life.

Shy One

Sweet shy one if you only knew
just what you found, when I found you
we've both had pain as well the joy
I promise to you, you are not some toy.

I know you have fear, and aren't too sure
But I swear to you, my feelings are pure
There have been many, this I admit
But now there is ONE, we are a perfect fit.

We haven't met yet, but quite soon we will
And when we do, your dreams I shall fill
I'll fill your days with the biggest of smiles
And all your nights with the sheets left in piles.

You've made me calm, you make me happy
I only hope this poem isn't too sappy
I want to sit with you and stare at the moon
I can hardly wait to talk with you soon.

Sight

When I see the full moon
Behind a veil of thin clouds
I recall my heart and soul
They open and I have sight.

When I am greeted
By fields of wildflowers
Amidst a sea of green pasture
I smile again and I have sight.

When I see the sunrise or sunset
The reds, oranges and yellows
So brilliant that they startle me
I waken once more and I have sight.

When I think of you
I am warmed to my core
I am enraptured by the depth
And I am no longer blind

I have love and it gives me sight.

Small Town Life

Endless miles of black asphalt,
Picket fence-like barriers,
Heat rolling upward in waves,
Concrete ramps beckoning to respite.

Golden Arch oases calling,
Portals to the aging towns
Of rotting wood exteriors,
And belted by greenery.

The equinox brings and takes
Life from these necessities,
For they live in opposition,
To the garish facades of cities.

People leave these places,
But are never gone from them.
They provide the stability
From the chaos they flee to.

Smoke

Ever watch smoke
Curling from the lit end of a cigarette?

Free and sensual, floating where it will
Letting the aimless currents of air
Move it this way and that

Much like my life
The universe moves me in so many ways
That I still don't understand

But I, like that smoke, let it direct me
Where I'm headed matters not
Where I have been, dictates my acceptance
Of this path

The road to freedom

Snobbery

So I'm not good enough
For your circle of friends.

You're right...I'm better.
I'm good enough to share
With people who matter.

Good enough to care
About those who want
To grace me with their association

Good enough to be grateful
For the gifts I have been given
By whatever power you believe in.

I have a great distaste
For closed communities.
They are populated
By closed minds.

Bask in the glory
Of your little group
Of little people

With little minds.

I prefer the company
Of the real world.

Someone Farted

He pictures her
A tiara of wild flowers in her hair,
A smile as radiant as the midday summer sun,
The body of a goddess.
Perfection in perpetual motion.

Then the weeds appear.
The dresser becomes a cosmetics counter,
His closet space shrinks by 93.6%,
once a month, she becomes a devil with an attitude.
Someone Farted In The Garden Of Eden.

She pictures him
A knight in shining armor,
Strength personified by dignity,
Stoically intellectual and philosophical.
The man of her dreams.

Then she hears the squeak of rusting steel.
She splashes down because he leaves the seat up,
His idea of a gourmet meal is pizza with everything
And he snores like a gorilla in heat.
Someone Farted In The Garden Of Eden.

They picture themselves together
Running together across a field of poppies,
Strolling hand in hand along the avenue,
In front of the fireplace on a snowy evening.
Harmony, peace, comfort, warmth. LOVE.

Then reality sets in.
He always forgets to take the trash out,
She whines about everything,
They argue about whose turn it is to do the dishes,
Feed the dog, vacuuming the carpet,
His dirty socks on the floor,
Her pantyhose on the shower curtain rod,
Her ex, his ex, her mother, his mother,
Chick flick or action/adventure movies,
His golf and her shopping.

Someone Farted In The Garden Of Eden.

SUMMER

You're a package to behold
A blend of fiery sensuality
And wide eyed innocence
That belies the honed business sense.

You can stir me to a frenzy
With that wistful promise
That only an Aries woman
Delivers without spoken word.

The me that knows better
Begins to evaporate in your climate
And you absorb me like so many others.
Fire heats air and stirs passion.

Beware too, of the illusion
I am not what I immediately seem either
for the same things that you mask
live within this shell also.

Look past what you do
To who you are
Set that free for a moment
And the mountain is yours.

The passion that you project
In ten minutes of song
Can be far surpassed
If you allow it of yourself.

One day soon, you will decide
It is time to bridge the gap of years
And explore the open wildness
That truly exists beneath your surface.

The poet writes of love
But does not live it
He exists for the chaos of moments
Much like the dancer.

That Which Is Within

Within each of us is something special
A place of pure, white goodness
It is in this non-judgmental space
That finds no ill will, no pain, no hate.

The size of this space is determined
By the strength of will given us.
Irrespective of size, it exists surely
As the sun rises and sets.

Rarely is another truly given access
And even that access is limited
By our own fear and insecurity.
Even we don't give ourselves all of it.

We speak the words far too freely
And then suffer the consequences
Brought by that misspoken term.
This place is a place of light, be spoil it not.

Do not be afraid of giving something
Of that space to another, as long as,
It is something shared in fact.
For it is only here, that love is borne.

The Act

Simultaneous acting
One act on stage
Another in the audience
Dancer works player & vice versa

Who's got game?
Who's lame?
Who's to blame?
No one finds fame.

Girl attempting to scheme
Player living the dream
Neither as it may seem
An altogether sad scene.

At the end of the evening
Each will find their way home
Continue their real life
And await tomorrows replay.

The Challenge

You challenge me.
Not because you are unattainable
But because you are Bright.
The challenge is for me to meet your pace.

You stir my soul
With your zest for life.
You see gems and gold
Where others see stone.

You draw me into the flame
With your passionate quest
To reach beyond complacency
To the stars of the Cosmos.

You re-awaken my senses
By being you, strong and knowing
Making me stretch and reach
We soar together, Hawk Like.

The Children

It was so very long ago
Life was different and easy
Dad worked, mom stayed home
And we were children.

It was safe to play in the park
To ride your bike, to daydream
We went to school and ran with friends
After all, we were children.

Then the assassin came
And a little innocence faded
But we moved on and forgot
Because we were children.

We began to hear of places
With strange sounding names
Saigon, dien bien phu, ia drang valley
But we were still children.

When they called us to go
We went like our dads and heroes
John Wayne, Randolph Scott, Audie Murphy

We were their children.

Then we learned fear
A constant black pall
Saw things no human should see
Death began to visit the children.

We lost lives daily
Worse yet, we took lives daily
There was pain and blood
Blood of children.

Life became of this second
There was no tomorrow, only now
And we can never forget, we grew up
Never again to be children.

The Field

The sun shines brilliantly
Even though there is still
A slight chill in the air.

The dew adds a whitish patina
To random spots in the field
Of deep green before me.

To my right trees form
A barrier wall, fence like,
Protecting something hidden from view.

To the left a hedgerow
Separating this field
From a twin.

I stretch, feeling the stiffness
Vacate my body and give
Way to the flexing of muscle tissue.

I reach and draw my weapon
And test its readiness
To join the battle that looms.

I hover at the ready,

Coil as a spring tensing
Preparing to snap.

I uncoil in a single,
Almost fluid, yet manic
Motion swinging the weapon.

And the focus of the weapon
Flies into the air,
Unjoined from its resting place.

It virtually soars
Into the open sky
Screaming silently.

And comes to ground,
Bouncing several times
And comes to its resting place.

In the reviled sand pit.

Sometimes I hate golf!

The Flame

This feeling that is growing
Helps me to understand that
It is as it should be
Moving from infancy to adulthood

Like a campfire built in the woods
Starting slowly, just smoke at first
Then, smoldering and glowing dimly
Soon reaching small, flickering flame

As fuel is added slowly and continuously
The flame grows to a soft but warming fire
That warmth can last if care is taken
And the fire tended with thought

We both have experienced the overwhelming heat
Of the fire built and fed too fast
Starting at a roar and becoming uncontrollable
And ending in the same way. Cold, spent ash.

We began that way, but apprehension
Slowed each of us at the same time
I think we both needed more
It is time to travel a different path.

Yes, those moments were exciting,
Coupled together, writhing
The heat of our passion,
A wildfire of sensations

Unspoken, we each slowed the other
And began a journey at a walk
Learning the other as we travel,
And another bond began to form

The glow is here now
The flame is beginning to flicker
We have discovered the warmth of friendship
And both know, the fire can roar

The difference today
Is that we are more in control
Of how it expands
And the passion is joined by other fuels.

The Forest

A summer walk in the forest
Awakens the sleeping senses
If you listen

Hush……..Hear the wind singing
Through the leaves – Gods Song

See the verdant brightness
Of the moss, sensually caressing
Upward along tree trunks
Brilliant greens against sturdy browns

Feel the crisp crunch
Of tan, dry Pine needles under foot
Mother Earths richly napped carpet

Smell the Camphorated Clarity
Of Fresh Air – produced
By natures purifier

Taste the freedom of a world
Living and Osmosing
In perfect harmony

The Human Condition

The human condition amazes me.

Yesterday I caught myself
Watching a couple in another car.
They were obviously a couple,
And I felt a twinge of envy.

I recalled the feeling
Of having that special person
Sitting next to me
And I remembered that warm glow.

I pondered that feeling
With some sadness
Allowing the loneliness to
Wash over me.

I wallowed in that
For a few seconds.
Then, it disappeared.
For I remembered
An argument and anger.

The trigger for that recollection
Was when the woman

In the other car
Stepped out, shouted,
And gave the guy the finger.

Maybe we weren't
So special after all!!

The Poets Reflection

Anger – Joy – Love – Fear – Sadness
Just emotions

We experience all of them
All the time

But for some reason
We can't seem to write about all of them
We seem stuck on just three
Anger, Love, Sadness
And they blend together

Like, "I'm so pissed that I loved you
And you hurt me
Now all I do is cry"
And THAT'S bullshit

On any given day
I laugh at my own and others stupidity
Something scares the shit out of me
I get mad at things that are fucked up
I fall in love all over again
And I cry about pain, mine and others

It makes me want to wax poetic and say:

I am so fucking pissed that I loved you so much
And yet you hurt me.

I'm laughing at myself
For being so stupid
As to cry for so long
And being afraid that you would leave.

I'm glad that truck ran over you!!

The Restaurant

Watch the wait staff
in a busy restaurant
insanity in motion

Hustle and Bustle.
get the order right.
SMILE - no matter what!

Drinks, appetizers, entree, desert
can I get anything else for you?
was everything ok?

geez, that guy at 3 is an asshole.
wow, the woman at 8 is drunk.
gawd, that kid is a pain in the ass.
no tip - it figures.

is my order up yet?
will you PLEASE bus 4?
what are you doing tomorrow night?

Going out to dinner!

The Ride Home

The palette is 4 aisles
Of asphalt, split by
Dotted white lines
Scarred by fleeting rubber tread

The artists are countless thousands
Of freedom seekers, mounted
Upon steeds of steel
Bearing a single "brand" – HD

Their song is a thundering roar,
A cacophony of sound, unique
To the breed, increasing in volume
As throttles are rolled open

Their inspiration is one
The 100 year celebration
Of the sire of their mounts
A Gathering of the Brotherhood

There is no question of
Geographical, racial, religious,
Generational, financial or

Social affiliation

There is only the recognition
Of commonality of the
Spirit shared within
This microcosm of a macrocosm

Hundreds of thousands of
Voices joined as one,
Singing one song
And painting a portrait of history

The Ride Home

The Ride

See the horizon afar
Fields and forests at your sides
The Hawk circling above
Shrubbery a blur of green

Hear the song of the road
The roar as road warriors pass
Voice of the river as you cross
The rush of air as you pierce it

Smell the freshness and the scent
Of days life welcoming you
Of foliage as it breathes
Of the highway tar and rubber

Feel your freedom now, today
Tomorrow luring you forward
The wind in your face
Roll life's throttle open, and ride

The Road

Living the freedom
of the black ribbon
of highway split only
by a wavering, fading yellow line.

Wind stinging your face
at 75 MPH, cool, hot.
Hair streaming, bike screaming.
Power beneath you, in <u>your</u> control.

At THIS instant
This slice of time,
<u>YOU</u> have the power
you OWN your life.

You feel the landscape
as much as see it.
You sense the wind
Driving and flowing away.

It doesn't matter
where the road goes
You are leaving it behind

along with the rest
of life's shadows.

    Live to ride
    Ride to live

The Rock

Yes, I can be cold steel.
I can be north wind harsh.
I can drink high octane
And piss pure flames.

I can turn my back and walk
Or I can stand and face demons.
I can take your heart
I can steal your soul.

I fear nothing – almost,
Other than my heart.
So, I expose little of it
And I am safe and secure.

In my fortress of self
I am defended and strong
Inured to the arrows
And protected – from myself.

The Sea

At Dawn, white foam topping green/blue glassine walls
Trade Winds coaxing the walls onward
Toward the shoreline

The swells build to a crescendo
A roar of strength and power
And then Diminish until they lap softly
Against beige glistening sand

Almost as if longing to creep further
And yet, seemingly trepidatious
Of the white granular texture
Of the beach

At night the foam presents a green phosphoric glow
And beckons the weak to join
With Her – Mother Ocean

The Universe

I have been told
More times than I can count
That the universe provides.

I tend to agree with that.
But I also think
The universe tests me.

It provided me
With a woman who loves me.
That I can't love back
In the same way.

It also provided me
With a woman I loved.
Who couldn't love me back
In the same way.

Somewhere within that
Polarized state
Lies the perfect relationship.

If I pass the test
The universe will provide.

The View from Here

Look beyond what you think
That you see – this is but a shell.
Can you see into my soul?
For that is who and where I am.

Trust your heart
Listen to your soul
Use your eyes to look
Into the being and not the mask

You seek the truth
And words do not speak it
A shared secret foretells
Of knowledge and truth – not spells

Do not fear – for I am real
I give you who I am
Nothing to conceal
This is my gift – it is me

Time to Listen

It's time for me to say something
That I should have said long ago,
Rather than to allow myself to
Bury myself in guilt and pain.

Your entire life has been dedicated to
Blaming everyone else for your failures.
When you didn't get what you wanted as a child,
It was your parents fault.

When a toy was broken, someone else did it.
When you scraped a knee, another pushed you.
When you were denied, dad was a bastard
When you failed, the subject was too hard.

In adolescence, she won because
She was teachers pet or had help
Your boyfriend cheated because
He was an asshole

As an adult, your depression was because
You were adopted, even though
You were loved by birth and adoptive
Parents who adored you.

And when we were together
It was because I manipulated you.
I lured you into loving me
And I dared love you back

When we split, it was my fault
Because I made you listen
To the truth about your escapism
And reality is ugly, stark honesty

You struck back and escaped once more
By killing the only thing left to bind us
In doing so you began my life
For now I appreciate what I was given

And you can go back
To blaming everyone else
Because your life has been fucked
By everyone but you.

Time

Tomorrow does not exist
The cost of waiting for the future
Is far too high for my taste
Time is far too dear

Yesterday is a cheap memory
It is gone and forgotten
Too many miles have passed
Too many bridges crossed

Today is my gift
This moment is all I own
NOW is the legacy of my life
A second past is a second lost

What could have been is nothing
What should have been is a void
What will be is secreted away
What is – IS

Traveler

9,000 miles from home
The Southern Cross a memory
Never forgotten, it holds you.
Fear not, these skies too hold wonder.

A new life beckons to you
You are welcome here
Not for what you do
But for WHO you are.

Your interior matches and exceeds
that physicality of you.
And each compliment one another
Creating the magic of self.

Your gifts set you on this path
The road lit by the circumstances
That brought you to this place

See the North Star
Sister to the Southern Cross.

Sonny

Sonny dying of cancer
he's lived a lot in his 60 years
while booze and drugs occupied him
he never assumed a loser persona

he was a commercial fisherman
owned a bars twice, lived in a dozen places,
did 10 years Hard Time
and is my friend.

he was our company handyman
even though the beast ravaged him
stealing a lung, flesh and his colon
his heart is huge and unstoppable

we laughed and bitched together
I watched his eyes glow over his son
listened to a million tales and jokes
and when he is gone I'll weep

but not for long..........
he will be with me forever.

Truth

Why ask if you don't want to know?
If the truth can set you free,
Why do you run from it?
Honesty requires courage, Fear breeds lies.

Do not fear the darkness
It hides nothing
Embrace it and be OF it
Then see the truth within

That which lies within your soul,
Reveals the silent beauty.
Strength beyond your comprehension
the ability to be the tower.

Find this and the need to ask is gone
All fear dissipates into vapor
Behold the wonder of you
When the truth lights your path.

Two as One

I watched them walk together
Hand in hand
Looking in store windows
Yet seeing nothing

Both were smiling
Lost in that remarkable oblivion
Alone together
And enveloped in each other

Their world at this moment
is a macrocosm
Of the microcosm
That is the essence of emotion

The totality of melding
And osmosing of
Two separate entities
To create the essential third

For all love relationships
Consist of three
One, another
And both as one

Wait For What

You say you can't see me
until you have
your "baggage together"

Interesting phrase, BUT,
what the hell
does it mean?

That I should wait
for a healing that
never comes?

That some strange
and mystical epiphany
MIGHT take place?

That your numerological "9" year
will be over
and that magical "1" year begin?

Or that I will
process then past
and forget about you?

I have
and I won't

Waiting

You watched from outside quietly
Observed all of my foolishness
Knowing that I would learn and change
And you waited for my growth

Did you know that I too was watching?
Did you recognize how I looked at you?
Did you not see what I truly wanted?
Or that I was waiting for you

What I write for you is different
Each passage comes from within
They aren't words on parchment
They are a portrait of what I feel

I've tried to tell you in many ways
To expose what is truly here
You listen and stand at the edge
Accepting one stanza at a time

You say you have no time for love
I say I have no love for time
Somewhere between those poles
Is what we both are waiting for?

Let's take one step forward
We have nothing to lose
We've held destiny at bay
It's time to stop waiting and start living.

Watching And Waiting

Watching and waiting
What is real, what is fantasy?
Caught in the vortex
Of wanting and wondering

Watching and waiting
What will be learned?
Are we trapped beneath
The wings of adversity

Watching and waiting
Where can it go
Is this a beginning
Or marching in place

Watching and waiting
Frozen in time
Letting life pass
What road do you take?

The moment is here
To step into tomorrow
End the watching and waiting
And walk into the sun.

We

We've known each other for a while now
Shared some moments, and a lot of each us
With one another, almost daring to be different
We got past the "club/customer" very quickly.

We each sense something else in the other
Neither knows what, but we both enjoy it
A bond of sorts grows, and we gingerly explore it
Baby steps in a budding friendship.

Last night was different, in a good sense.
We, as always, explored a dozen subjects
But something else pushed to a new plateau
I don't know what, I don't analyze, I just experience.

I like the way you challenge my thinking
You like that I listen to you
We both like this level of comfort
And the ease in which we can trust.

In some ways, I think you are older than I
In other ways, you seem comforted by my experience

Science calls this a Symbiotic relationship
I simply find joy in it.

We're Pregnant!

How I love to hear the sound of your voice….
Like the screech of fingernails on a chalkboard!

The way you spoke softly when awakened…..
What the fuck do you want NOW??

The way you shared the glow of impending motherhood…
I'm SICK goddammit, you expect me to COOK??

And the memories experienced together, as ONE…
See how YOU like pissing every 5 minutes!!

How we melded as partners, joined in bliss….
I'm TIRED after 4 hours of Judge Judy, all you have to do is work!

Ahhhhh…we reveled in the miracle of being parents….
I have hemorrhoids, a sore back, raw nipples and a fat ass – HELL YES I feel just fucking gorgeous!!

I Love You
It'll be a cold day in hell before WE do IT again!!

What We Are

We were friends, remember?
I was seeing your roommate,
Before you were roommates.
I introduced you to her.

Then you and I began to share
And we each found something
In the other, that fit like a glove
And still, we were friends.

It grew quickly, we spoke of it
Like we were in control
Yet, there was something else,
Hidden by both of us, unspoken.

I was attracted to someone
And you disliked her, reasonless.
I liked another, and you called her a child.
The friendship was changing.

I didn't understand why, because,
You called us "friends"
Then your dad came, and he liked me.

And told you I was the one for you.

You dressed for my tastes
And said I was your best friend
And that was the way relationships
Should begin, as friends.

Now you hate the others that
Catch my eye, or who look at me.
You found a reason, for me not to see
Anyone else there, or anywhere.

What has this evolved into?
Where is it going?
Are we friends? Are we more?
Can we have it all?

It's up to you to decide
But let's not dance the dance
Let us speak our minds.
More importantly, let's speak our hearts

What He Discovered

He discovered that
There was much more to life
Than simple existence
It is more complex than that

He discovered that
Life was meant to be lived
At full speed, with intent,
With attention, with passion

He discovered that
He could not help someone else
Find that life within them
No matter how badly he wanted to

He discovered that
In order to discover life,
One had to suffer and rejoice
And sing their own song

What He Felt

Joy - Joy in everyday life
in holding a child and watching them laugh
in seeing a field of green
dotted with wildflowers, against blue sky

Anger - Anger at the worlds wrongs
at peoples lies and ignorance
at their lack of responsibility
at the injustices confronting him

Fear - Fear of not completing life's tasks
of not being up to the challenges
of not meeting expectations
of being alone and exposed

Love - Love of life
of being born, near death,
and being born again
of being able to love

What He Forgot

He forgot the freedom.
That pure freedom of being alone
Unfettered by life's restraints
Responsible only for his own life.

His entire being had been spent
Concerned with what others thought,
Felt or believed of him.
He had allowed himself to buy into that.

Now he knows
That this hell was self induced
This was not what others expected
It was what HE expected of himself.

How, why or when it began
Has no relevance worth contemplating
For the rebirth and awakening
Brings the same freedom

As Springing from the womb.

What He Gained

For a very long time
He thought he lost something
He thought everything had been taken
He was wrong

He had gained
He gained perspective
He could look at the world
And see beauty instead of bleakness

He gained reality
The reality that each has an independence
That each has unique views, needs and wants
That each heals from within

He gained truth
The truth that his love
Had to be for himself first
Before he could share it with another

He gained his life back
He has no fear of sharing it again
He gained the knowledge
To share rather than give

What He Remembered

The smell of freshly mowed lawns
Drifting on the wind.
The aroma of sawdust and Lucky Strikes
From his fathers shirt.

The comforting warmth of the kitchen
When his mother was holiday cooking.
The sweetness that enveloped him
In his grandmothers touch.

The anger that seethed at his siblings
Incessant needling and teasing.
And the glow of pride that arose
When he protected them from bullies.

The joy at being surrounded
By an overwhelming love exuded
By the entire family
Father, Mother, Grandmother, four brothers, one sister

Eight individuals, one common soul.

What He Saw

He saw much in his life
He saw the beauty in the world around him
Forests, oceans, prairies, deserts
each singing their own unique song.

He saw so much love
it is everywhere
a mother holding her child
a bird feeding its nestlings
Lovers holding one another
a mare nursing her foal quietly.

He saw the darkness too
The hideous brutality of war
The callous nature of abusive people
The bleakness of depression
Death, destruction, hate, despair.

More than anything else
He saw himself
and how everything, everyone
is a part of what makes him who he is.

Good and bad.

What He Thought

He thought he knew sensation
He had experienced many
Pain, joy, agony, love (or a reasonable facsimile),
Anger, disgust, ecstasy.

He thought he knew people
He had met many
Philanthropists, philanderers,
Jocks, fun folk, assholes.

He thought he knew women
He had been with many
Soft, harsh, needy, lonely,
Enticing, stubborn, sensual.

He thought he knew love
He had felt it often
Caring, protective, concerned,
Comforting, warm, enveloping.

Then he met her
and discovered in a very real way,
that among all his other assets
he really didn't know shit.

What He Wanted

To laugh with his friends
To share his joy and pain with them
To find a new friend – every day
To see the beauty in all things

To make a child happy
To watch them smile
To take away their fear and pain
To marvel as they grow

To see and hear and feel and taste
To be of the world, not just in it
To understand what others feel
The be one they can share with

To love another as they loved him
To want to hold them as they held him
To be able to set them free
To revel in his own freedom

What I see in you

As intriguing as you are,
As mysterious and mystical,
I still see into the depths
To the softness inside.

You revel in creating wonder
But long for someone
To genuinely look beyond
And accept rather than control.

You cannot stand constraint
Freedom is your trademark
Those who attempt to bind you
Are treated with contempt.

Be wild and free like the wind
Whipping your flames higher
Do not give up that liberty
It is what makes you – you

What I Want

What do you think I want?
Only for you to see WHO I am,
Because, when you see that
You will know what YOU want.

What you see in my eyes
Is what has been missing
From your life,
No pretense, pure honesty.

I ask nothing of you
Other than for you to be YOU,
No veils, No Image, No Expectations.
Put those away for those who need them.

No, I am neither blind nor stupid.
I have no NEEDS other than Oxygen
For I am at peace with WHO I am.
I live, I soar, See me.

What Is Sought

What is it that I seek?
Why do I keep searching?
If I can't even identify
What it is that I want?

The biggest problem
Is that this picture
Constantly changes, evolves
And then dissolves.

I thought I found what I sought,
but it was transitory, a dream.
For when I had it, it was wrong
And I wanted something different.

I intensified my search, diversified,
But still, the goal was unclear
A blurred, amorphous mass
And I kept looking for something.

I became surrounded by what
Many think is perfection
But quantity is not quality

And while there are many, there is not one.

I have an inkling that what I seek
Is not out there in this world,
That I look in the wrong places,
Perhaps the answer is right here…..in me.

What Will It Be Like

You are heaven to hold in my arms.
I know, for I held you last night
As I slept, you crept into my heart
And lived in my dreams.

I felt your warmth against me,
The silkiness of your cheek
Against my chest, your breath
Warming me, inside as out.

To know that two became as one
And that we were together
Even though apart
Is bliss beyond words of the poet?

While this distance blurs my view
It does not exist in my soul
I feel your hand in mine
And our energies are joined.

When our mouths do meet
They will already know
For they have been together

And will be again.

When We Need

When we feel down and it seems so bleak
We seem to find each other
And color our lives with something more
A bond is being forged by the universe.

When we are happy, we have learned
How to share that too
We talk, and laugh and cry together
It seems we share many lessons.

Everything happens for a reason
Our reason just waited until
time was right, and healing begun
and we were ready to step beyond.

So here we are, closer than the miles,
Leaning and supporting, sharing and caring
Looking forward to the next moment
And savoring the present.

When You Are Ready

When you are ready, call me
Perhaps I will be there
And perhaps not.
I refuse to play the game.

A player I am not
My path is a different one
Gamesmanship is for weaklings
Boys who know the taste of fear.

My strength is my intensity
For I face the unspeakable
With the knowledge of my lineage
If you fear that, then flee.

I'll not wait for your call.
As my spirit leads, I will follow
Unabashedly, Unashamed
For I want, I do not need.

Where Did It Go

Where did it go??
It was here for what seemed
An eternity, never-ending,
Stretching days into eons.

It was my constant companion
Always at the forefront
Always stabbing at me
Always in the way of progress.

I hated it
I wanted it dead and gone
I wanted it to move away
But I feared letting it go.

It made me ill
It tore at my guts
Ripped flesh like a claw
Squeezed life from me.

And then one morning
It was gone, it was silenced,
It was banished into nothingness

And I was free.

I was comforted, warmed,
And calm for the first time
In as long as I can remember
No pain or anger.

I had no hunger or longing
No remorse or regret
The lamp had been lit
And I could again see.

And it was gone.
Vanished, vaporized
No, not love, that was reborn.
In myself, for myself.

It, was the sickness.
The ailment of self indulgence
And the healing had begun
And would become whole

As I have.

Where Does It Come From

Poetry does not come from a pen
Or from ones head
It comes from within
From your heart and spirit

It is not reflective of school
Or a large vocabulary
It is the mirror of your soul
It is a true image of you

The words you write
Speak not only of others
They paint the picture
Of the depth that you feel

Which Face

I detest having to read between the lines
Or look beneath a mask of words.
Say what you mean, mean what you say
Quit hiding under the cover of falseness.

We all do it, some in the name of diplomacy
And some to avoid demonstrating fear.
But yet others do it in avoidance,
A way to disguise and deceive.

Sometimes what is said is not as important
As what is not said, and we miss
What might be, and what might result,
If only we had spoken truly.

Uncover your soul, speak honestly
Not thoughtlessly, not harshly,
For these words cut far more deeply
Than the skilled surgeons knife.

Who Am I

When I was asked
Who I am, I had to ponder the question.
What I am was easy.

I'm a biker, dressed in Black,
Rolling the power on,
My steed a masterpiece,
Of Glossy Black and Chrome.
Pointed at the horizon
Direction irrelevant.

I'm a technology professional,
Understanding high tech theory and practice,
Implementing applications to benefit the user,
Making the impossible probable.
Enabling voice and data connectivity
Across cities, states, nations and foreign lands.

I'm a hetero male.
Testosterone driven and pheromone stimulated,
Marveling at women's breasts, butts and thighs,
And the eyes, oh my God, the eyes!
I love the way our maker put Eve together
Perfect symmetry, poetry in motion.

I'm an educated person.
Two BA's and an MBA,
Lover of art, music, writing.
Two fisted drinker, one line delivery specialist.
A brawler, a lover, jack of all trades,
Soldier (once), Jock (always)

Who am I?

I'm ME, with all of life's contradictions!

Why Do I Get Up So Early

Why do I get up so early you ask?
To greet my rebirth

Each and every day
Provides me the opportunity
To make a fresh start
To be the best me that I can be

The universe greets me
With a smile in every golden sunrise
It says to me, "You're ALIVE,
Now LIVE"

I figure that if the universe
Cares enough
To smile so brightly on me

Shouldn't I return the favor?

Why

If we were meant to be sad all the time
Why is the sky Azure Blue
Why is the sun so brilliant
Why do we have eyes

If we aren't supposed to experience joy
Why does the robins song lift us
Why do we long to hear a lovers voice
Why do we have ears

If we were designed to feel nothing but pain
Why does a child's hug feel so sweet
Why does an orgasm make your toes curl
Why do we have nerve endings

If crying is our natural state
Why do we laugh so hard at jokes
Why does your heart feel so full at a simple glance
Why do we love

And if all there is, is gloom
Why does music exist
Why is art beautiful

How can we write poetry?

Wild and Free

During these bone chilling
Days, housebound and fenced by snow,
I long for warm days and nights
Wild and free, wind in my face.

Seated astride this steed of steel
Bright sunlight glistening
Against flanks of brilliant red
And the reflection of sparkling chrome.

Tires singing against beckoning highway
Backed by the throaty serenade
Of tailpipes playing the tribute
To the power beneath me.

This is the time I wait for each year
The time when ice and wind chills
Are moments of history, and my soul
Is alive, wild, and free.

Woman of Fear

Woman of fear, woman in pain
What do you think I wanted of you?
Did you think that I wanted to own you?
Did you think I was like the rest?

Where did you think my tears came from?
Where did you think my happiness came from?
Is it possible that I had no ulterior motive?
Is it possible that my love was real?

Can it be that I truly cared?
Can it be that fault never mattered?
Was it true that past mattered not?
How can it be that I only wanted to share?

I spoke the truth, told you no lie
But it was too much for you
And you made our love die.
We said our goodbyes and they will last.

I have a new life just as you do
My pain is gone, replaced by indifference
For what we had is in the past
Woman who was, woman who seeks.

Creatures Of The Night

Is it real or a mirage?
You float before me, diaphanously exotic
Fear or adoration?
A little of both perhaps.

Those azure eyes burn through me like lasers
My heart threatens to stop at one moment
Then to explode in the next
Are you doing this, or am I?

The hand reaches out to me
But I cannot touch it
It evades my touch
Yet tempts me to extend to it

I beg for this moment to last
I know that it won't
Each time you appear, you escape again
Exactly like you did in my waking hours.

An Exquisite Moment

An instant in life
3:08 am, I awake with a start
alert, disturbed by something
and I see your eyes

Somehow you came to me
We both know why but are afraid to speak it
I asked you what time you thought of me
And you froze, knowing that I KNEW

Our dynamic has shifted
What once was jibing kinship
Has become something else
Its nature undefined but known

Soon we shall speak of it
We will step gingerly toward it
For we both fear
That which has wounded us both

There are eons between us
Oceans to be crossed
But at the right moment
Your eyes will be the bridge

Seasons

In October, I watch golden leaves float
Lazy escape from their summer home
Nimbly evading the shore and floating objects
Finding their rest to become the fodder for future growth

In January, ducks and geese walk on it
Taking a rest in their journey to southern breezes
They preen and dine and gather to avoid solo flight
A crystalline path leading to regeneration

In March, it reflects angry purple skies
It swells and surges, rushing and rising
Streaks of lightning mirror on its surface
Constantly in motion, it shows its power unstoppable

In July, swirls and eddy's welcome denizens
Two, four or more legged, all sharing its respite
Cool me, feed me, comfort me in thy motion
An endless journey to meet Mother Ocean, the beginning of all

Your Answer

You asked me a question
You want an answer
Other than "I don't know".
My response may not be what you want.

Do I believe in love?
Yes, but not as most do.
I don't believe in love
As an everlasting emotion.

I believe we fall in love
In time slices, parsecs
Momentary lapses in reality
Passion, white hot, a flash.

And as it comes, It goes.
What was us, becomes one,
Pain replacing warmth
And typically lasting longer the love.

Do I love you?
I love this moment,
I'm not sure that I

know what love for another is.

If I suddenly discover it
I'll tell you, but do not expect
To hear those words from me
Anticipate hearing that I like you.

For if there is such everlasting.
All encompassing feeling,
Then merely saying the words
Is not nearly the honor it deserves.

Your Name

Jackie, Jacqui, Jacquie
You are as enigmatic as your name
You puzzled me, even when you agreed
Does she or doesn't she?

Then, a small light comes on
No answer is a positive response
Your integrity requires you to stop
Only that which is wrong

That which is right needs no answer
Only the room to grow
Only the time to be what it will be
Keep it inside until you are ready.

It is far better to have questions
Than it is to have all the answers
For without the questions
There are no dreams to be realized

I don't pretend to understand
The mysteries held within your soul
The paradox of your name

Is the portrait of your being

That knowing smile, a small touch
Erases my doubts, clears that fog
And another piece of the puzzle fit
Stay as you are, intriguing one.

Night

Riding east, watching the horizon
It begins to turn from purple to blue
The golden glow of a new day
Looms in the distance

The air is cool & damp in anticipation
We will stop, and like vampires,
Enfold in each other to sleep
Until nights shadow comes again

Our night is the day of others
While they go through the motions
We are wrapped in each others safety
Hidden from their eyes, we find solace

Our flesh together, momentary urgency
Until, sated for now, we sleep
Comforted in the others arms
Until we wake and ride again – into tomorrow.

Our Path

Each of life's journeys
Begins with a single step
Our first step took time
And our journey has just begun

Along this path we walk today
We will stop to enjoy scenery
Expect a distinct lack of pressure
For the path is one to be savored

What will be, will be
What there is today
Developed over a year and more
Sunrises & Sunsets, Days & Nights

Let this flower blossom
At its own pace
For one rushed or hurried
Can never fully develop.

Patience

Patience. It even sounds boring
It's only a couple of letters
Away from a hospital stay
Yet, without it, we would not be.

Fortunately, you had patience
And so our song begins
You waited and watched
Until you saw my time had come

I have so many gifts
But patience is not one
And now you hold me in check
Teaching me that time provides

I will learn this lesson
For I am unwilling to allow
This moment in time to pass
Ignored and unrecognized

I am here and will stay
I will not be deterred
Or have my vision blocked by others

For I cannot let you slip away

We had it happen in eons past
But the universe offers once again
This time my eyes are open
And I have patience.

Siren

70 MPH – Roaring into the sun
pipes singing the cacophony
of the roads sheet music
tires caressing the avenue of tomorrow

a slight twist of the throttle
brings the power beneath you
to life, the vibration stirring
beckoning for the feed of fuel

the horizon coaxes us into it
promising to provide new vistas
painting on the palette of life
calling my soul forth – seeking

the pull of that force
is irresistible – a sirens song
as surely as this calls
I respond, as did Ulysses.

When Did You Know

When did you know?
Did something change the way you felt?
Was it already there, but dormant?
Or was I blinded by other things?

When I first read your words
I saw one picture, a surface view
but then, the next day as I re-read
the picture evolved, and my heart soared.

Those words are always with me now,
My own words can hardly describe
The depth and breadth of emotion
That you have brought to life.

At this moment in my life
I have but one single wish
and that is to bring you
the happiness you have given me.

You like Blunt?

You say you like blunt
How blunt do you want?
I want to be with you.
Is that blunt enough?

No, I don't mean I want
To sit and visit for moments
Interrupted by unwelcome ears
Visited by uninvited guests.

I want to have long talks alone
I want to know YOU
I want to share all with you
I want to let you know me.

A walk along the shore
A quiet dinner for two
A movie, play, concert or gallery
A ride through the country

Holding hands in the moonlight
Laughing at life's foibles
Bitching about work

Learning life's lessons

Time together
Time alone
Time to live
Time to grow

Learning to trust
Eliminating fears
Erasing doubts
Yes, it's blunt, and honest.

Your Work

I love watching you work
Carefully choosing who to tempt
Knowing which will succumb
And which will earn your disdain

Few are worth your concern
You hate the lies and deceit
Most are here and gone again
They cannot touch what is YOU

You feed their dreams
But you know it is not a filling meal
It is an empty list of promises
A diaphanous veil to keep them hoping

But what does it do to you?
Does it make you wonder
Where fantasy ends and your life begins?
It meets today's needs, but leaves you hungry.

Possessiveness

You get angry because I have no jealousy
Your choices are yours
Yes, I believe in your dreams and hopes
I have mine too

I have no desire
To possess you
My satisfaction from the moments
That we share together

Give me only what you will
I refuse to put you in a cage
I love the wild, free bird
As I love my own freedom

I will give you what I can
I can no more be bound than the wind
My spirit is unfettered
We together are the prairie fires.

Recollections

Lying together in the morning
The memory of last night
Lingers in the air and in my senses
You stir my soul.

The caress of your breast
Brushing against my arm
The soft silky sensation
Of your thigh, leg draped across mine

The scent of your hair and perfume
Calls to me, drawing me forth
The warmth of your palm
Softly stroking my chest

The slow, deep sound of your breathing
Is the sirens song
That encompasses my being
In THIS moment, this morning.

What Is Love

What is Love?
A timeless question that has been answered
In countless ways, and I have no idea if any are correct.

Sometimes, I think there is no such thing
Only the firing of certain neural synapses
That occur when one body is held against another

When the ocular nerves are stimulated
In a certain manner, when specific pheromones
Are secreted and receptors accept them readily.

When the ear drum vibrates in particular way,
And flesh meets chemically compatible flesh
There is a spark, ignition occurs.

And we are "in-love"
Whatever that means!

What Is Happening

Today, at this moment, something is happening.
I think that you know it too
For, last night, I saw it in your eyes
And felt it when we touched.

I don't know where it is going,
That gift is not mine, and I'm glad.
I would rather follow the path as it runs.
Let what will be, be.

I do know that the universe drew us here
For a reason, at the same time, in this place.
We have already brushed against
Our own admissions of attraction.

I used to come to this place
To see several friends, and share a moment
Suddenly, my desire to be there
Is fueled by a want to talk with you.

Imagine the forces that came together
For this chance meeting to occur
One guided by the North Star

One by the Southern Cross.

I choose not to force this, but to wait
And let fate weave the material
Of what becomes of this pattern,
This patchwork tapestry of lives.

Changes

Squirrels are scurrying storing food
Horses coats are thickening and bodies fattening
Fields being denuded of crops
Burrows being dug by the dozens

The trees donning their autumnal cloaks
Of brilliant red and fiery orange
Pumpkins and squash filling the supermarkets
The sky filling with honking geese, southbound

We put away our cutoffs and swimsuits
Jackets become the uniform of the day
Stacks of split logs begin to appear
And frost emanates from us as we walk

And as the ghosts and goblins begin to make their rounds
And deer appear more frequently
I welcome the change
And will curse the cold another day!

Crystal Dreams Publishing
Is proud to present these other great authors

Phillip C. Beebe
A Stab in the Back
Beyond the Edge

Jack W. Ward
Shadowlands Theater

Sylence Campbell
Sounds of Sylence

Nicole Givens Kurtz
Browne Candidate

John Harrington Burns
First Bite
Hidden Treasures

And many more

Crystal Dreams Publishing
PO Box 689
Dover, TN 37058
USA

crystaldreamspub.com
P.O. Box 698   Dover, TN 37058

Crystal Dreams Publishing

Order Form

Quantity	Title/Author	Price

Subtotal $ _____

Shipping and Handling _____

$2.50 US, $3.50 International 1st book. Add $1.00 for each additional book.

Total $ _____

☐ Enclosed check
☐ Please bill my Credit Card
   ☐ Master Card _____
   ☐ Visa _____
   ☐ American Express _____
   ☐ Discovery _____
☐ Money Order

Note:
A physical street address MUST be provided. All books are shipped via United Parcel Service (UPS). UPS will not deliver to PO Boxes

Merchandise will not be shipped when paying by personal check, until the check clears. Returned checks will be subject to a $25.00 returned check fee.

Mail to:
Crystal Dreams Publishing
PO Box 698
Dover, TN 37058